IT HAPPENED NOW WHAT?

How to Move Beyond the Pain to Take Back Your Power!

Kimcherian Johnson

ISBN 978-1-63844-574-6 (paperback)
ISBN 978-1-63844-575-3 (digital)

Christian Faith Publishing, Inc.
832 Park Avenue
Meadville, PA 16335
www.christianfaithpublishing.com

Requests for information should be submitted to:
Kimcherian Johnson
kimjohnsonempowers@gmail.com

Printed in the United States of America

DEDICATION

This book is dedicated to every person that has experienced trauma, loss, and pain that has left them unable to move forward. I am your voice.

CONTENTS

FOREWORD

It Happened, Now What is a testimonial book that we are overcomers, through Him that loves us. As I methodically maneuvered through each page of Kimcherian's book, she was transparent. She shared many very personal and intimate details of her life as a young girl and becoming a woman.

What was most revealing and impactful to me was in the earlier chapters of her life how some of the same challenges that she encountered mirrored several events of my life. Much like Kimcherian.

I also experienced the rejection felt of not having affirmation and the love of one's biological father in their life, to learning just how to survive the streets that teach and give you the ungodly game plan of how to survive life! As with anyone who has faced challenges, one would be able to relate to the struggles of finding a lasting resolution to life's challenges.

Lastly, Kimcherian reveals how she turned her life around through being affirmed by God and learning how to trust her heavenly Father and what her worth is to God and His kingdom. It just goes to show that we may never understand why we seemed to have had to go the long way around; nevertheless, grace was there even when we didn't recognize it.

My spiritual daughter Kimcherian's book, *It Happened, Now What?* is a must-read for the believer and unbeliever alike; it will bless you!

Apostle Harold K. Browning Sr.
Pastor & Founder, Faith Mission Ministries, INC
and Global Network of Christian Churches (GNCC)

ACKNOWLEDGMENTS

To my Lord and Savior Jesus Christ, I owe my life. With Christ, I can truly do all things, but without Him, I can do nothing.

To my priest and king, my earthly everything, Elder Maurice Johnson, I honor you as my husband, best friend, and partner in ministry. Thank you for being there.

To my spiritual parents, Apostle Harold K. and Prophetess Gwen Browning, you facilitated my healing process. I am forever grateful for your love, leadership, and guidance.

To my parents, children, grandchildren, family, and friends, your love and support have lifted me as you could never imagine. I appreciate you.

I would also like to thank my editors, Laluye Tadanyigbe and Ashley Richardson. Thank you for your support through it all.

Introduction

When a car accident takes place, many thoughts run through one's mind. The first thing one tends to consider is dialing 911. The next may be to get their phone out and take photos, or grab their license and insurance information. The driver might get out and check their vehicle for damage, if they can move, that is. And if the accident is more severe, one might have no option other than to remain still until the first responders show up.

After the police have done their investigation and the first responders have finished their examination, the tow truck has come and towed the vehicles involved and the cleanup crew has removed all debris; the accident is over.

Or is it?

Often, when we are involved in an accident or experience some traumatic or tragic event, we don't immediately call 911 or cry out for help. The desire to seek spiritual help isn't always our first response either. What we do is go into survival mode. We may be stunned or in shock, but we tend to keep it inside and seek an immediate way out on our own. After the storm has been calmed, we might physically move from the scene of the accident or trauma, but we might never fully recover mentally. If not dealt with, the experience becomes a bad movie replaying in our minds each time we are triggered.

Life is rife with encounters that we'd rather not have. We experience tragedies, disappointments, and crises in real time; and when the dust settles, the sirens stop, and everyone has gone home, we remain at the scene of our pain. Not necessarily physically.

These incidents make us question who we are, who God is, what life is, and what our part is in the world, resulting in a collision of our expectations and the realities we are forced to endure.

I want to introduce to you my younger self—a little girl that had the odds against her right from the start. I encountered hurt, pain, mental and physical abuse, rape, and prostitution all because I had no idea who I was. I made many mistakes and repeated many of them, trusted in people that let me down, and sank to my lowest multiple times. But God shall get the glory at the end of this story.

Fall and *autumn*—two words used to describe the same season. It was my favorite season and also my worst. On one hand, I loved how the wind brushed against my cheeks on a windy day; and on the other hand, I hated how the dead trees reminded me of myself. Hollow on the inside but full of color on the outside.

"If you want to know what we're doing, come in and see."

Those were the last words spoken to me before I learned to run without direction. This book is for those who have experienced or are connected to someone with trauma, hurt, and shame. You've run from it, covered it up, overcompensated for it, and hid it; but it's time to face it, release it to GOD, and declare your victory over it.

Whatever your "it" happens to be, there is nothing bigger than the cross. It's time to get free so you can help someone else get free.

CHAPTER I

Family Pile Up

My earliest memories are of me jumping in excitement at the sound of my father's Volkswagen Bug coming around the corner. He was a baker that worked nights and came home around ten or eleven every morning. It was the highlight of my day to see him step out of the car and grab his lunch bag. I would scream from the screen door, "Daddy! Daddy!" as I ran to receive an embrace (I would give anything today to see him drive up, and although I am forty-eight, I would still yell "daddy").

I could tell he was tired but he would crack a smile at me, perhaps because he was grateful to hear how excited I was to see him. But the smile only lasted a few minutes. His face would lose that glow when he would begin to talk with my mom and soon he'd lie down and go to sleep. I didn't get to see him smile much, but I appreciated what little I got. It was worth it.

He was a man of few words to many and to us at home. He was a very private man, too, but he had a funny side to him which I only got to know about after his death. "He was a funny man," "Oh, how he loved to tell jokes," they said. What I saw and knew was a man that worked hard. The only other thing he showed any passion for was watching baseball and coaching Little League baseball—which was difficult for me to understand because as far as I knew, he had a temper and had very little patience. Perhaps that was why he was mostly quiet at home and spent most of his time there watching baseball, baseball, and more baseball.

He liked Andy Griffin, The Jeffersons, and Fred Sanford. He would sit and watch and not move or talk. But when he laughed, it was so contagious and open that you'd forget he was a disciplinary and so capable of keeping secrets. He had secrets.

I never saw him and my mom display affection or say "I love you" to each other, but I believe they loved each other in their own way. I loved him deeply too. I loved the fact that he worked hard to keep a roof over our heads and provide for us. When I got selected for the girls' basketball team, I had to get basketball shoes which cost sixty dollars a pair. He bought them for me—my first basketball shoes.

So I guess it was only natural that I sought his validation. It wasn't very often but the times I felt the proudest were when he'd come up to my school to see me play in the games or play the drums at one of the local high schools. It meant the world when he'd look at me and wave. It made me feel like a daddy's girl knowing I had his attention and admiration. I knew my mom was always present, so I did not have a yearning to have something special with her. But with my dad it was different.

I was an overweight child and that bothered him. And it bothered me even more, hence the hunger to build a connection with him. My desire to be acknowledged and accepted by him was strong. Unfortunately, I felt like an embarrassment to him more times than I felt like I made him proud. And I wished I could fix it.

The thing that bothered me was I wasn't in charge of feeding myself. My mom cooked three meals a day, every day. Cooking gave her purpose and was her way of showing love. That may be why I got large portions. I loved to eat too, so I didn't say no if I was offered seconds. She was such a good cook and when I ate, I felt most loved by her.

I was overweight. I wasn't able to run and play with other children. In fact, my mom kept me away where only she could see me. I was practically raised as an only child. My best friend was my dog, Gus, a huge Doberman who liked no one but us.

My mom was strict and overprotective of me. I would learn years later why. She had had to deal with a lot and she never spoke about any of it. I only saw the effects of it. I saw depression, anger, and anxiety. I was too young to understand it.

I guess she did what she knew to do. I still admire her ability to maintain a spotless home, cook to perfection, and ensure my perfect grooming. But as a child, my hunger for attention lingered. While I wanted hugs, kisses, and laughter from her, I longed for attention from my father. I wanted him to notice me, tell me he loved me, and spend time with me. But we don't all get what we wish for, do we?

There is an old saying: "Curiosity killed the cat." It may not have killed me, but it definitely triggered my first collision. The effects of the wreck caused me to spiral downward at just ten years old.

My family had moved out farther in the suburbs to the upper-middle-class side of town. The area appeared safe and seemed to be a great place. Even my mom was so comfortable that she easily made friends with our next-door neighbor and other families around. The area was truly like a breath of fresh air. Or so we thought.

One evening, the neighbors next door invited my mother to play cards. She took me with her. I hadn't made any friends yet so I was quite excited to just get out of the house for a bit. The lady of the house was a nice woman, just around my mother's age. She had a teenage son who was upstairs with two of his cousins, both boys. In the downstairs den was an elderly woman who was their grandmother. I was told to sit downstairs alone with her while the mothers played.

Soon, the alcohol ran out. The ladies wanted to go to the store to get more. I was told to remain with the grandma while both moms left for the store. In retrospect, I should have done just that. Sitting there, hands folded on my lap and bored out of my mind until the moms returned would not have killed me. But I heard the boys laughing upstairs.

At this point, curiosity introduced herself to me in the questions that rang through my mind and the overwhelming desire to know. What was so funny? Why were they laughing? I could go see right?

I quietly climbed up the stairs to go satisfy my curiosity. At the door, I yelled, "What are you all doing in there?" One of the boys cracked the door open and said, "If you want to know what we're doing, come in and see."

I was hardly in the room when I heard the door shut and the lock turn behind me. I didn't know it yet, but that was the start of my collision. Because next thing I knew, I was struggling under the weight of one of the boys as he forced himself on me and raped me. They covered my mouth with their salty hands, suppressing my screams, and, for what seemed like a lifetime, they took turns to violating me. All three of them.

Then like a police siren they heard the sound of their parents' car coming uphill and got off me quickly saying, "You better not tell your mom. She is going to kill you and we will say you are lying!" "You shouldn't have been up here anyway." I put my clothes on as fast as I could and ran downstairs shivering, scared, and numb all at the same time.

My mother started calling out to me immediately as she entered the house. I responded, "I'm here," and complained that my stomach was hurting bad and I wanted to go home. She asked me to just lie down on the couch and I'll feel much better. I did but came back after a while insisting that I was not well. Then we left.

It was the longest walk of my life. I'd just lost who I was—my innocence. As the wind brushed against my skin and the leaves danced to the rhythm of the breeze, I screamed inside. I was devastated beyond anything I could understand.

It felt like I had just experienced a three-car pile-up. I actually did. It was a hit-and-run, and I was left in a pool of guilt, shame, and embarrassment. I got home, and before I could take a breath, I realized not only was I feeling sick and afraid, I was injured. This trauma had started something in me, physically, that I was too young to experience or even understand. The only thing I could think was, I have to suck it up. I have to keep it in. I have to survive. I became a track star—running from what had so suddenly become my reality.

CHAPTER 2

Running into Danger

Growing up as an only child was pretty lonely for me. Most of my friends at school had siblings, or they got a chance to spend time with each other outside school. I did have a brother, but he lived in another state. I only got to see him on summer breaks. It didn't help that my mom kept me secluded most of the time.

We moved to Lithonia, Georgia, and there I met my first real friend, Sarah. She was a Caucasian girl. Her father had committed suicide years earlier, leaving her mother in a perpetual state of depression. Sarah's mother didn't really approve of me and Sarah being friends, but because we were so close, she tolerated me. It didn't bother me. What bothered me was the one at home.

I felt suffocated, especially by my own mother. She had become more and more moody and angry. There were clearly things going on with her but I never knew what. She would take these afternoon naps and when she woke up, she would be angry and yell at me over nothing. It was as if she hated her life. Years later, I would find out she was an alcoholic. She drank beers throughout the day and was perpetually hungover, especially after waking up. Most times, she complained of headaches.

Years later when I went to counseling to help me deal with many things I had experienced, I shared about my mom. I explained to the counselor her moods and what I had endured. The counselor asked if she was an alcoholic. I said no, she just drank beer. That was when I learned that beer is alcohol. Before that, I had no idea that beer was considered alcohol and the side effect of drinking daily was an alcoholic. But I could relate. My mom had used alcohol to help her get through life, as I had used food to do the same thing.

Back to my friend, Sarah, and I. Sarah was a fun and cheerful person. She had a beautiful smile and was easily the life of the party. I liked that we had quite a lot in common—we both liked the same kind of music and had the same fashion sense. I found it funny that she had no rhythm, though. Sarah couldn't dance to save her life, but she was my friend and I loved her. But I also envied her.

Sarah had way more freedom than I did and it made me jealous. She was free to do stuff how she wanted and when she wanted with way less policing than I got from my folks. She was even skipping school to hang out with boys which I, too, wanted to do. So I started skipping as well until we both got in trouble. This only infuriated my mother the more. And it only made me want to escape it all the more.

I was young. All I wanted at the time was to break free from the pain I was feeling inside because of home. My mom never asked me about how I was feeling or what was going on with me. She only wanted to correct me when I was wrong and make sure I was doing what I was asked. It made me livid. I felt trapped. I felt unloved. So I decided one day that I was going to skip school and spend the day on my own terms—to have a taste of true freedom. I left home on the school bus, went to school, left school early, and caught the Marta bus heading downtown Atlanta.

I never spent a lot of time downtown because my mom didn't give me the chance. The closest I ever got was to Fourth Ward where my aunt lived. And now I wanted to soar on my own.

I ended up downtown with my friend at a pool hall that was in the basement of a building. There were video games, people playing pool, and dimmed lights. It seemed like a cool place. As soon as Sarah and I walked in, all eyes turned to us. I don't know if I had ever had that sort of attention on me before. It made me uncomfortable and nervous but at the same time, I felt liberated. Besides, I was with my friend. Sarah introduced me to some friends she knew there. We had loads of fun. I didn't want this day to end but we had to get back in time before the bus left for home.

As soon as I got home, I felt trapped again. I felt like a bird that had escaped its cage and was now walking right back into it. It didn't help that my mom was consistently getting on my nerves, just like my dad was. I had no voice. It did not matter what I thought or felt.

I had enjoyed that one day of freedom downtown with Sarah. I kept wondering how good it would feel to be free every day. So I decided that I was leaving and not coming back this time. Like the last time, I went to the school by bus, left, and caught the Marta bus heading downtown to the pool hall.

When I got there, I recognized a couple of people that Sarah had introduced to me the last time. We said our hellos and hung out. That was when I really got to meet Stan.

Stan was one of the more popular guys around. He was influential around there and very much adored by the ladies, so he had them around as much as he wanted. I had met him the last time, but we had not exactly talked to each other. He came up to me and asked my name again. Then we spent some time talking, trying to get to know each other as friends. I thought it was so cool that someone as popular as he would have any interest in me. I was elated! But that was just because I did not know yet what exactly I was getting myself into.

Stan was very easy to talk to. Before I knew what was happening, I had already shared with Stan everything that was going on with me, my parents, and my plan to not go back. At the time, that was my state of mind and that was what I really wanted. In fact, I was convinced that that was what I needed. So one might understand my excitement when I heard Stan tell me that I could stay! He said I did not have to go back if I did not want to and I could stay for as long as I wanted; maybe forever. I was elated!

He called over some of the ladies that were hanging around there and introduced me to them. Then he said to me, "You can hang out with us." They were staying around the corner in a couple of hotel rooms which they told me they were more than willing to share with me.

I followed them to the hotel. All my life, I had never stayed in a hotel, so this was the first time for me and I was amazed. My new friends had two rooms. Two of the ladies I had been introduced to had one room to themselves and the other room had Stan and his girlfriend. Both rooms had two beds in them. I was to stay in the room Stan shared with his girlfriend—both of them took one bed and I had the other.

Needless to say, I had a great night—a free night. And the next morning I was in for more pleasurable news. We were all sitting around and talking when Stan suddenly said to me, "We need to take you out to get some clothes." I was stupefied.

"Really?" I asked, wondering if he was just pulling my legs or something.

"Yes. I will have some of the girls go with you so you can get a couple of outfits."

He was looking at me. Until that moment, I don't think I had ever felt so special before.

"We are all going out tonight," he added with a smile.

With that, I melted inside. I had never been out anywhere. And of course, no one had paid attention enough to want to take me shopping for new outfits. It made me feel so good, especially that they wanted me to go out with them.

By mid-afternoon, we were back from my little shopping spree. I'd found something to wear on our little outing later in the evening. I spent most of the rest of the day with the ladies. I noticed some crazy looks from a number of them once or twice. I was beginning to feel uncomfortable knowing that they were talking about me behind my back, but I summoned the courage to ignore it. Perhaps I was seeing something where there was nothing, I told myself. So I concentrated on what exciting new experience the evening held for me.

It was finally evening. Stan told us ladies to go ahead, he was going to meet us there. I did not know where there was, but I got dressed along with the other girls and off we went.

So there I was, walking down Auburn Avenue with these ladies, totally clueless as to what lay ahead, but going to it anyway. It was getting dark now and we were still walking. Soon we came across some guy standing by a building. One of the girls said, "I got this," walked over to the guy, and went behind the building with him. I didn't understand what was going on, so I asked immediately where she was going. The other girls laughed at me.

I asked again. Then one of the girls got irritated and said, "Listen. I don't know why you're acting like you don't know what it is. We have to work and you will be working too. Ain't nothing comes for free. Those clothes you got today, you got to work for it. She went to do what she needs to do to get this money for the family and you need to do the same."

My mouth dropped. I was terrified, but at this point, I felt I had no choice. This was the price I had to pay for freedom. My heart was beating so fast I could barely hear the men as they drove by whistling to us.

I was not dressed provocatively enough to draw a lot of attention, but one car came close and its driver called for me to come to meet him across the street. The girls looked at me, and one of them said, "You better go. Just ask him what he wants. It is twenty-five dollars for a blow job, and fifty dollars if he wants sex." I walked across the street shaking inside, walked up to his car and got in the front seat. He was a young man, maybe about twenty years old.

"Hello," he said.

"What's your name?"

I was still in shock, but I managed to say my name and he told me his.

"This is my first time doing this. How does this work?"

I would have sworn it was me talking because those were the exact thoughts in my head, but that was not my voice. It was him talking.

I looked at him, "Really?"

"Yes," he answered. "I am a college student and I have not done this before."

"It's my first time too."

I must confess, it boosted my confidence to know that I was not the only first-timer in the car. I asked him what he wanted; he said he wanted a blow job. He gave a few directions as to what exactly he wanted and in the end, he paid me and dropped me back off at the corner.

I stood there, still in shock, but all I wanted was to get back to the ladies and Stan. There was a small bar across the street where we were supposed to meet up afterward. I got in there and went upstairs. I could not see the ladies anywhere, but I sighted Stan very easily. I went to him and told him what I had just done. He was about six feet, two inches tall, so when he hugged me, looked down at me with a smile on his face, and said he was proud of me, I felt like a little girl making her papa proud.

"Do you have the money?" he asked me, still smiling.

I handed it over to him and when I saw how pleased it made him, I too felt good. I was so thirsty for approval and validation that for a moment there, I felt that I had just done something right.

When the ladies got back, I told them, too, how it had gone. I thought the night was over and we would head back home, but it had only just begun.

We all took a cab to another side of town, Stewart Avenue, which I would later learn was a quite popular spot for prostitutes. We just hung around and I watched as cars sped past us. Some cars honked, some drivers made comments, and others stopped. One by one the ladies were being picked up by customers until I was the only one left.

Then I saw a car across the street and a man asking me to come over. I went across and got in the car. It was an older man; he looked to me like he was in his late thirties or early forties. Overweight and very demanding, he did not speak to me kindly at all.

He drove me behind a school. I was afraid, but I was more disgusted at his mean spirit. He ordered me to get in the back seat, got in with me, and began to take his pants off, telling me to do the same. Because of his size, he could not maneuver the way he wanted in the back seat and that got him mad.

He was finding it difficult to get on top of me and I could not get on top of him either. He resigned to just get a blow job and ordered me to give it to him. I was so disgusted that I wanted to die and throw up at the same time. He saw the fear and disgust and yelled at me. I got right to it but was saved by the blue lights of the police car that had just pulled up behind us.

He was hysterical. He yelled at me to put my pants on, while he tried to put his on as well. The officer came up to the window and asked, "What are you all doing back here?"

"We're just talking, Officer," the mean man answered.

"Just talking, huh?" The officer shined his lights on me.

"How old are you?"

"Eighteen, sir," I lied.

The officer looked at the man again. "Get out of here. And I better not catch you all back here again."

We both got out of the back seat and got into the front, and the man started driving. He stopped on the curve and yelled, "Get out! And I ain't giving you shit!"

I watched as he sped off leaving me there all alone. I was hurt, disgusted, feeling dirty, ashamed, belittled, and wondering, "What am I doing? This is not my life."

There was something inside me that was saying this is not you, but there was also something that reminded me that I had nowhere else to go. There was no safe place to land.

I got back to the hotel but was too afraid to tell them about my experience. I just told them I didn't get anyone else. It was too embarrassing to let them know that I messed up and didn't get the money. The experience had drained me, and I was so exhausted, broken, and wounded. I don't even remember how I fell asleep.

Early the next morning, there was a loud knock at the door. It was the police. Stan told me to go into the bathroom, step in the shower, and close the door. The police asked Stan if there was a young girl there, and he said my name. Stan said there wasn't, but the officers came in and searched the room. They found me in the bathroom standing in the shower, took me out, and put me in the vehicle.

For a moment there, I was relieved. But quickly I realized where I was going back to, and all I could think was, *I don't want to go home. I don't want to go back to the hurt that I left.*

After my parents got me and realized I was fine, they were angry and upset. They yelled and asked why, but no one thought to check and see how I was doing inside. No one thought to send me to a therapist or pray with me because prayer was not a part of my home.

The fact that I was back home now did not change anything. Life just went on like it always did. But I had changed. I was changed since that day in my tenth year when I was raped. My outlook was filtered. All I saw was survival and running. I would run away two more times. The third time ended in me getting pregnant.

CHAPTER 3

Accidents

I got pregnant with the first person I actually consented to have sex with. He was a nice country guy that was three years older than me. He got caught up in the issues that I had at home, so he agreed to help me when I wanted to run away from home again. I planned to move in with my brother in Florida. I'd live with my brother and my boyfriend could come to visit me in the summers. It was such a great plan.

The thought of living with my brother made me feel like I was close to real happiness. My boyfriend was a funny guy. I was happiest when I was with him and it meant a lot how supportive he was. It was on the trip to Florida that my son was conceived. My plan to live with my brother didn't quite work out because his mother called my parents and she had to take me back.

It was heartbreaking for me that I was again going back to the place I was so desperately trying to run away from. My mom and dad gave me the blues when I arrived. They had been so worried when they realized I was gone and now that I was back, they were hurt that I had tried to run away again. But even that did not change how I felt. Even I had no idea how I was feeling. All I knew was that I needed to get away from there. They did not understand me and I needed to escape all the heat. I ended up leaving again for the ump-teenth time.

This time I was hanging out with some college girls. They were obviously more experienced than I was. So when they told me they thought I was pregnant, I was shocked to my marrows. I took their advice and had a test done to confirm and, thinking back, I had never prayed for something to not be true as much as I prayed as I waited for the result.

It was positive.

I cried so hard. I remember thinking that even though I was running away, I needed to call my mom. I had no idea what she would say. I just needed to hear her voice.

I had been gone about a month by now. I put the call across and took a deep breath as I waited for someone to pick it.

"Hello?"

"Ma."

"Kim? Is this you?" I could hear the surprise in her voice.

"It is me, Mom."

"Oh, Lord!" She gasped. I could tell she knew something was wrong. She paused for me to speak.

"I'm pregnant, Mom." I expected a lot of reactions, but what I got was definitely not one of them.

"Okay. It's gonna be okay. What are you going to do?"

I allowed the tears to flow freely at this point. Then I told her the truth, "I don't know, Mom. I don't know what to do."

"Come home. Please come home. I won't bother you, I promise. Just come home and let me help you."

I did just that. I went home, and for once things were different. My mom showed love and compassion toward me. She helped me in any way she could and for the first time, I felt truly at home.

I was sixteen and about to be a mother. I knew nothing about having a baby. And since I was just a clueless teen, I had to go to a teen clinic in the downtown area for care. I lived in the beautiful suburbs but had to catch the bus to go forty-five minutes downtown to the clinic.

The nurses were not kind at all to any of us. They felt that we were just "fast-tailed" girls out there spreading our legs to anything that said hi. They would give all of us the same appointment time, and there would be a line of us—all twenty-five of us. We would come in, give our urine specimens, get weighed on the scales, and have our vital signs taken. All the while, the nurses would shake their heads, yelling our names and making us feel like the scum of the earth. It killed me every time.

The whole thing frightened me greatly, the idea that I was going to be a mother, I mean, especially as I was not prepared. Who would be prepared? The day after my son was born, as he slept in his crib by my hospital bed with the most peaceful look on his face, the nurse who kept coming to check on us finally stopped and looked at me.

"Have you picked this baby up?"

I looked at her with all sincerity and said, "Well, he is not crying. He isn't bothering me, so I thought I shouldn't bother him either."

"No. You have to hold and bond with your baby."

To bond? I had no idea what that meant. I had never bonded with anyone, so I didn't understand what I was supposed to do. I picked up my baby and held him in my arms. But it did not shrink my cluelessness or the large chunk of fear stuck in my throat.

I was six months into my pregnancy when I met him. My baby's father and I had broken up. This man was nice and friendly. He showed interest in me even though I was pregnant and was more than willing to help. And I was more than willing to go with him.

I was in that place where I wanted to leave home again. My mother had been there for me when I needed her the most and I was eternally grateful for that, but at this time she had lost the sweetness. She was trying so desperately to control how I raised my son. I, too, was trying to avoid having to have my boy experience the kind of childhood I had. As a result, there were lots of clashes and it was just not working out.

Consequently, I was glad that I had him, especially as he was willing to step in as my baby's father. The way I saw it, he was an opportunity for me to leave home and never have to come back if I didn't want to. Besides, I was in love. Or was I, really? Looking back, I don't think I knew what love was, or if I was even capable of recognizing it and giving it back. But when he asked me to marry him, I did not hesitate to say yes.

The fairy tale didn't last long, though.

When I became his wife, he became overly possessive, extremely jealous, and wanted to control my every move. He didn't like going out and being around people and preferred to just be at home and be intimate. I wasn't comfortable with that and let him know how I felt and for that, he began to curse at me and call me every name but my own. He would cut me off from everyone and tell me nobody cared about me. He would verbally abuse me and then follow up with an apology and sex. He frightened me to my marrows.

I will never forget when he first became physically abusive. We were arguing and I was trying to move past him when he blocked me, picked me up as they would do in wrestling matches, and slammed me hard on the ground. He knocked the wind out of me, and I could not move. That was the day I became terrified and realized I had only moved from the frying pan to fire.

I had nowhere to run this time. I couldn't go back home, so I just dealt with it. I genuinely felt as though that was what I deserved. The physical and mental abuse continued for years. I loathed myself for not having the guts to leave, but I had to remind myself of the truth—I had nowhere else to go.

Five years in, I decided to end my life. I had had enough and thought I did not have the strength to take any more. I took my son to his godmother's house for the weekend and planned to down a whole bottle of pills. I just wanted the pain to end.

I placed the pills on the dresser and stared at them until I burst into uncontrollable tears. I cried so much because I was just tired. All my life, all I did was run, and now I was out of air. There'd never really been a safe place for me. There was too much hurt that I knew for sure I was incapable of bearing and I just wanted it to end. As I sat there in my own pity party, summoning the courage to not desert me now that I wanted to do something brave for once, I suddenly remembered this woman I had met the previous day.

I had gone to the beauty supply shop to get myself a relaxer for my hair. As I stood there comparing one brand to another, I heard a voice behind me, "Hello. You're so pretty."

"Thank you," I said as I turned to face the most beautiful smile I had ever seen.

She was a graceful lady with a beautiful face. A younger girl was standing beside her.

"I would like to invite you to come visit my church." She was still smiling.

I had never received that kind of invitation before. I had been invited to parties and hangouts—invitations that I mostly wished I had not honored. But a church? This was a first.

"Okay," I said, trying to return the smile.

She was excited. "I know you will love it. We are all family."

She gave me her phone number and said she looked forward to seeing me there. What was important to me was that she noticed me. She even said I was beautiful. That was what I chose to remember. I forgot the rest.

But as I sat there on the bed, the bottle of pills looking back at me from the dresser, I saw her face again—her smile—like it was calling to me and extending that invitation a second time. I cried out. I was tired and I told God just that, exactly how I felt. I expressed the pain I was feeling, the hurt in my heart, and the sadness that clouded my days. Then I decided to give it one last shot—I told myself I was going to go to church the following day. If I felt nothing afterward, I was going to resign myself to the fate I now believed was mine—the pills on the dresser.

The following morning, I got dressed, set out on my way, and pulled up in front of this small white church. There were cars parked everywhere and even though I was outside, I could hear loud singing and praying coming from the building. For some reason, though, I felt a chill I could not explain. I was afraid. I considered turning back for a minute but decided to stay when I remembered the promise I made the previous day. I sat in the last row at the back and then the preacher came up to preach.

There are moments in life when you are overwhelmed with the events unravelling around you so much that you begin to tell yourself that it is not real, maybe you are dreaming. This was that moment for me. Because as the preacher preached, his suit soaked wet with sweat, he paused, looked around, and began to say the oddest thing.

"You are in this room. God sent you here today. You've been raped and abused and you want to end your life. But God sent you here today. Come on to this altar."

I was in shock. I began to weep uncontrollably. The lady sitting beside me understood why I was crying and comforted me, and then she encouraged me to go on to the altar.

Slowly and full of shame, I stood up and made my way to the front. I knew people were looking and it took everything in me to not turn around and run out. At this point, every bad thing that could possibly happen to me had already happened as far as I was concerned. If this was going to make all the pain go away, I was willing to walk down that aisle a thousand times more.

I don't know what I was expecting but when I got there, he began to tell me exactly what I had been dealing with. He laid his hand on my head and began to pray at some point, and all I know is that by the time I came to, I was lying on the floor drenched in my own tears, worshipping and crying. There were other ladies there with me, each having their own experience.

As I lay there having the experience of my life, I felt a heavy weight lift off me. I felt God. For the first time in my life, I felt his comfort wash over me. I felt love and felt loved by him. I gave my life to God that day.

CHAPTER 4

Collision

The great thing was that I had changed. My marriage? Well, let's just say I couldn't say the same for it. My husband was no kinder; he continued to be mean, abusive, and hurtful.

By now I had made some friends in the church. I tried to share with them what I was enduring in my marriage but they told me that God did not like divorce. They advised me to stay in my marriage and sort things out. That only confused me even more. How on earth was I supposed to do that? How was it even possible that God wanted me to remain in a marriage where I was constantly being hurt?

I decided that I wanted out. It was no longer safe for me to remain in a place where I could end up dead the next minute. My husband was away working with the military at the time so it seemed like the perfect time to leave. I planned my exit but as they say, man proposes and God disposes—my husband's father passed away.

I felt so sorry for him. It was certainly going to take him off the edge so I decided to be there for him as a support system. He asked me to accompany him to the funeral. How could I say no? I was empathetic. And for the very first time since we got married, he was vulnerable. So I let my guard down. We ended up making love and a few weeks later, I found out I was pregnant.

This was the last thing I expected, or even wanted. I began to console myself with the thought that perhaps this was going to soften him up, if not completely, then at least to a considerable degree. But I was wrong. Just like the hundreds of times before this one, I was wrong and he only became more controlling over me while he lost control over his temper.

When I got pregnant by him, I thought he was going to change. It excited him for a while, but before long the jealousy and abuse came peeping through the cracks and looked me straight in the eye.

I remember one time when he kicked me in the stomach even though I was seven months pregnant. He snored badly when he slept and it disturbed me more than ever during the pregnancy, so much that I could not sleep. I would go to sleep in the living room because of this. One night, he woke up and realized I was gone. He came into the living room yelling and calling my name. I did not want my son to keep hearing the yelling, so I got up and went into the bedroom with him. He kept yelling at me in the room, drew his leg back, and kicked me on the stomach. I was so hurt physically and emotionally. Of course, he apologized and said he was sorry. But the resentment had already been planted and the guilt of allowing myself to get stuck again was just unbearable. I remained like that until months after my son was born, and then I started to remind myself that I deserved better.

There was something inside me that kept pushing the old me out of the way. A crack of light that gave a possibility to a new life—a new way. Even when I thought God had left me, I realized he had been there the entire time being a source of strength.

One evening, my husband and I got into another heated argument, and for the first time, my oldest son, who was nine years old at the time, saw my husband pushing me and he walked up to us, pushed him back, and screamed, "Stop hitting my mom!"

I saw the astonishment in my husband's eye and the fear that swept over me was not of this world. It was a different type of fear—a momma-bear kind of fear—because I knew what was coming. My husband threw my son into the closet and something just snapped in me. I went straight to the kitchen, grabbed a butcher knife, and came toward the bedroom.

In my mind, I was thinking, *You can abuse me. I walked into this death trap by myself anyway. But I will not let you hurt my son!*

I raised the knife aiming directly at him. He must have realized that I was not playing, so he attempted to grab the knife on the sharp end and it cut his thumb. That sent him dashing into the room and shutting the door behind him. Looking back, I am grateful to God that only his thumb got hurt because, to be honest, I was aiming for his chest. I had been abused long enough and like any momma bear, I would do anything to protect my son.

I went back to the kitchen and dropped the knife in the sink. Then I sat in the recliner and rocked. It dawned on me as nothing else had ever done: it was over and I had to get out. I called a friend and we planned my departure for the next day while he was at work.

I was on the run again. But this time, I knew I would never allow myself to be abused again. I was not alone—I had God and I had the people he gifted me. The Lord put a powerful woman of

God in my life. She was everything I needed. She welcomed me, nurtured me, and pointed me to God. Although my life took various turns here and there, and there were yet many more obstacles to climb, I was well on my way to now what?

42

CHAPTER 5

Who Am I?

Growing up, I never looked like anyone in my family. I did not think much of it, though, because my grandfather was light in complexion and my mom's mother was fair-skinned, too.

One time when I was forty-four, I was attending a birthday party when one of my relatives whom I had not seen in years embraced me and asked me to go into the bathroom with her. She was particularly happy to see me. I was glad to see her, too, but the excitement in her eyes was far more than just being about seeing me. She kept staring at me in the restroom. Her eyes screamed something to me which I could not understand, so I asked her what was wrong.

"It's nothing. I should not say anything."

Now I was curious, "It's okay. You can tell me."

"You look just like your real Mom."

I paused. No, the whole world paused, and I took a deep breath to steady my voice because I knew it was going to be shaky now.

"What did you just say?"

There were tears in her eyes now, "I don't know why they have not told you."

I was hungry at this point, hungry for information. Where was my real mother? This means I was adopted, right? What exactly happened?

I looked up to her and comforted her, "It's okay. Where is she now?"

"I have no idea. She used to live near our house, but at some point, I just stopped seeing her. Or you."

I still had many questions I wanted to ask her but people started coming into the restroom so we had to end the conversation.

Those few minutes changed a lot in my life and thus began my pursuit to find my biological mother. I couldn't stop asking, "Who am I?"

I reached out to the only mother I knew for the truth. The poor woman was caught off guard, and she denied it all. That hurt deeper. All I wanted were the facts. I just wanted to understand what happened and why. But she stuck with the lie, and when I realized she was not willing to discuss it at all, I became my own private investigator determined to find answers.

For a while I searched and searched for any helpful adoption information, asking more questions about my biological family. I found out from the local adoption that my mom had passed away nine years prior. I wasn't sure how I felt about that. A part of me was broken because I had never had the opportunity to know her or feel the warmth of her embrace; another part of me was relieved because honestly, I didn't know what to expect if she were alive. Would we be able to build a relationship now? What if we didn't get along?

Among the information I was able to dig up was the fact that she had me at 14. She had wanted to keep me and had tried to do so but could not because she struggled with drug addiction. But what shocked me more was the knowledge that my biological father had been a married man—a married man that was sleeping with a 14-year-old child.

It felt good to know that she could have chosen to abort me but decided not to. She tried, with help from her family to care for me for as long as she could. I was also excited to find out that I had a brother, aunts, an uncle a niece, and cousins—a whole other family!

But something else still bothered me—I was struggling to understand why my mom never told me the truth. It would take a while, but I would, through prayer, counseling from my spiritual parents, and love from my husband, later come to find peace and understand things from the viewpoint of my adoptive mother. Out of the many options she had, she chose me and accepted me as her own. She never had any children of her own, I was all she had. I believe she was protecting me from what she perceived as danger. Perhaps she thought the knowledge will break me to bits—she wasn't entirely wrong after all. I have come to realize how blessed I am to have been chosen. When you are adopted, you are chosen.

My mothers were not perfect but I believe that they both had perfect love for me. Even I, I am now a mother of five and I admit that I am not perfect. I haven't always gotten it right with my children, but the love I have for them comes from a perfect place.

I still wonder sometimes if what my biological mother went through, especially while being pregnant, has had any effects on me. Were my experiences a direct measurement of the things she experienced?

I now have a greater appreciation for women who give their children up for adoption and those who choose those who need a family. I have compassion for those who have been adopted because I am one. I understand that part of my ministry is to women who have experienced all this and then some. We must be able to see the purpose in our pain, to get the lesson to help others who face the same or similar situations. In the end, it's not just about what happened to me but how I used it to help someone else.

CHAPTER 6

Now What?

After we experience tragedy, we are left feeling fear, shame, guilt, hurt, and pain. Just as in an automobile accident, when we are hit our bodies respond. The muscles tense up depending on where we were hit and how hard our body has been affected. And we feel the pain.

Although we may have left the physical scene of the accident after a while, the effects can last a lifetime. We may become stuck on the emotional pain and the physical damage if we don't seek help. The feeling of frustration, the nightmares, the fear of driving again, and worrying about how to get another vehicle may enslave us and have us stuck in reverse. But the kind of stuck I am speaking of as it relates to trauma is the loss of focus, vision, or purpose. The loss of trust, especially in one's self, or the loss of one's identity in the chaos of the tragedy may have one feeling lost. There might be a desire to change but no direction or drive to do so—a complete cluelessness as to how to move forward.

But a sailor doesn't navigate with ease in the thickness of the night in confidence without a lighthouse, does he? And the clay doesn't mold into a beautiful vase by itself, does it?

> "For I know the plans I have for you," declares the LORD, "plans to prosper you and not to harm you, plans to give you hope and a future. (Jeremiah 29:11)

God, being our creator, knows the plans that he has for us. I never knew that my life wasn't just about how I wanted it to go. Never did it cross my mind either that perhaps I had a purpose, but I do have one. God never intended to harm me, but to give me hope and a future, the very one he intended for me all along.

When we find ourselves stuck in a terrible experience, the first step is to seek our Heavenly Father. He created us in His image and likeness and has a plan for our lives. He is our lighthouse; he is the Potter and we are the clay. And just as the Potter takes the clay with a clear picture in mind as to the work of art he wishes to make from it, God gives us breath with a clear purpose for us in mind.

However, sometimes things may go south. When this happens, there is no blame. Oftentimes when we are hurt, we look for someone to blame. Blaming only delays our healing process. Instead, learning the process of forgiveness is a better way to start healing. Once I repented and gave my life to the Lord, I embraced his love for and forgiveness of me. I received God's love for me and allowed his grace to wash over me. I began to allow God to heal me. I neither blamed my mom, my dad, the teenage boys, the pimp, and prostitutes, nor do I blame my ex-husband. I forgave the two men that I had to sell myself to. Instead of holding on to the trauma of my experiences, I became thankful to God for keeping me through it all. The only way to move forward was to cast all of my cares on the one who first loved me, the one who created me. But most of all, I had to forgive myself. I played a role which I admitted and chose consciously that I no longer would wear the title of victim.

The things that I have experienced and shared are not about blame. They are about not allowing myself to heal from one trauma, and carrying that hurt and pain into other areas of my life. I lost my identity so young and I continued to run and try to find it. I searched for love, validation, and acceptance. I searched for so long without finding that I always felt empty and alone. But my desire was just to see others happy so that maybe, just maybe, they would return the favor.

It was not about my mom. She had her own pain. She did what she knew—what she thought was best. She's had her heartaches and traumas in her own life. It wasn't about my father either. Perhaps he was satisfied with his life; perhaps he wasn't. He must have had his own challenges, fought his own battles, and had his own demons. We all do. But the point of sharing my experiences is to help us realize that no matter what, we must find our way to freedom and trace our steps back to the place where we ought to be.

Five Points to Working Through Your Healing

> And he said unto me, "My grace is sufficient for thee: for my strength is made perfect in weakness." Most gladly therefore will I rather glory in my infirmities, that the power of Christ may rest upon me. Therefore I take pleasure in infirmities, in reproaches, in necessities, in persecutions, in distresses for Christ's sake: for when I am weak, then am I strong. (2 Corinthians 12:9–10)

I have provided below the five steps that I took to freedom. These five steps will get you well on your way to healing and wholeness. Each step will challenge you, but when applied, things will certainly turn around instantaneously. You will no longer remain stuck in the pain of your past and will begin to take steps toward the purpose God has for your life. It's not about perfection but about allowing God's process to work.

Step 1—Seek the Father First!

Once we begin to seek our heavenly father and learn about the love he has for us, our healing process automatically begins. God showed his love toward us when he gave and sacrificed his only begotten son, Jesus. Embracing God's love for us causes us to want to love him back. It makes us want to surrender our lives to him. We realize that this life we have belongs to the Lord and so we should live for him. We are his workmanship, and so we should work for him.

> If you have not accepted Jesus Christ as your Lord and Savior, I admonish you to do so now. Here are two scriptures that you could read: (Romans 10:9)

> That if thou shalt confess with thy mouth the Lord Jesus, and shalt believe in thine heart that God hath raised him from the dead, thou shalt be saved. (Ephesians 2:8)

For by grace are ye saved through faith; and that not of yourselves: it is the gift of God.

After you have read the above passages, recite this: Lord Jesus, I repent of my sin, come into my heart, wash me clean, this day I make you my Lord and Savior.

And that's it, you're saved. If you have turned away from your relationship with God, all it takes is for you to ask God for the forgiveness of your sins. The Bible states that God is married to the backslider. So even when we turn from him, he never leaves us. Reconnect with the Lord today. Reviving your relationship with the Lord opens the door for healing and wholeness.

Trust me when I say, God is the only one that can make us whole. In Jeremiah 1:5, God says, "Before I formed thee in the belly I knew thee; and before thou camest forth out of the womb I sanctified thee, and I ordained thee a prophet unto the nations." This is true, and it only makes sense that the one who formed you has the perfect formula for your wholeness. He knows what makes you tick and how best to restore what has been broken, heal what has been wounded, and give peace where storms have caused unrest. We must seek God first for guidance, strength, and healing.

> But seek ye first the kingdom of God, and
> his righteousness; and all these things shall be
> added unto you. (Matthew 6:33)

All that we need can be found in the kingdom of God. We are not only seeking the King; we need to seek the kingdom as well and its righteousness—the right way of doing things. It's through Christ that we learn the right way to think, speak, and live our lives. It is the first step that will get us on the right track to healing. If you are still not sure about trusting God, I want you to know that it's okay. God knows right where you are, and he loves you so. He has a way of drawing us, like none other. There is a song called The Reckless Love of God by Cody Karns. This song truly speaks of God's never-ending love and the fact that he continues to keep coming after us. You should listen to it.

God is our healer and our deliverer. The way to start new is to surrender our lives to Christ or rededicate our lives to him. We are then open to receive love, the Word of God in our lives, and the Holy Spirit as our guide.

Step 2—Find a Safe Place to Land

Reach out to someone you can trust. Open up as the Lord leads and share what you are going through.

I was able to find a woman of God that cared enough to ask me how I was doing. She opened her home and heart to me and began to speak life over me. She also reintroduced me to Jesus because my first encounter with the Lord was not the best. Although the ladies at the church I had been to at first meant well, they didn't really attempt to educate me on the Word and the heart of God. But this woman began to show me in the word the nature of God. She also shared her personal testimonies of God's grace and healing over her life with me. She wanted to see me healed and set free. We prayed together and studied together. I called her home the house of refuge because it was the place where I was able to find peace. That place of peace helped me begin to get unstuck. That is why I say we must find a safe place to land because healing takes place in a safe environment.

But before any of that, the only true way to get unstuck is to first acknowledge that you are stuck. Acknowledgment is the key to release! To acknowledge, we must stop avoiding the truth or covering things up and allow God to have full access to our hearts. We must evolve into understanding we don't have to remain where we are.

The enemy desires to isolate you. He doesn't want you to feel loved or supported. He wants to get you alone so he can play old DVD movies over and over in your mind. He only wants to remind you of your past because he has no control over your future so that you can keep condemning yourself instead of seeking the help you need. When you make it a point to find someone you can share your heart with, you will feel comforted, heard, and encouraged. Be careful who you share with, though. There are people you would share your struggles with and instead of being a pillar of hope, they would further drag you under the weight of your troubles by planting doubt in your mind. The safe place you need, however, is a place to feel peace, love, and comfort, and receive wise counsel. And then, of course, we must check our connection.

We must check our connection to God. Are you praying, having devotion time with God, and studying the Word of God? It's not just about talking to God; more importantly, are you listening and obeying him?

It is important to check your support system as well. Ask yourself, have you been totally transparent with your spouse, parents, or close friends about what happened to you and how it has affected you? If you have not prayed and asked God for strength and talked to, someone you can trust and that is emotionally stable to handle your submissions, it will not be easy to do it alone. If you don't have anyone, seek counsel from your Pastor. I will have some resources available for you at the end of this book. I would suggest that you connect with someone as soon as you can.

Do not think for a minute that the kinds of people you surround yourself with do not matter. Are you surrounding yourself with people that keep you lifted in prayer? Are they people that see the good in you and have a desire to see you win? Do you have people around you that hold you accountable and are not afraid to hold you to your word?

Check what you listen to and what you watch. Are you listening to negativity or unfruitful things? Are you watching TV programs or browsing social media content that causes you to feel vulnerable, lonely or triggers negative behavior?

We must disconnect with anyone or anything that encourages our stuck status and connect with God and those willing to help us get unstuck.

Step 3—Forgive

As we ask God for forgiveness, we must learn to forgive ourselves. You cannot continue to beat yourself up over mistakes that you made when you did not know better, or keep reminding yourself that you are the scum of the earth when God calls you his own. In fact, the more we hold on to the hurt we caused ourselves and remind ourselves of the poor choices we made, the more we leave the door open for the devil to plant seeds of doubt in our hearts. Have I really changed? Has God really forgiven me? Do I have a right to fellowship with God? Should I not just forget about having a new start and keep drowning in sin, besides, what else do I have to lose? It is only at the point where we have forgiven ourselves that we can find true peace to move on. Forgiveness is one of the best things that we could possibly do for ourselves.

Then, as we learn to release ourselves from these feelings of inadequacy, we can move into the next phase of forgiveness which is forgiving those that have hurt us. Forgiveness is done by faith; it is not a feeling. At no point do we ever feel like forgiving the people that have hurt us. If anything, we tend to feel the opposite but we have to do it because it is not a suggestion from God, it is a directive. We must forgive by Faith. The feelings will come later, or not. Either way, we must forgive.

Holding on to the hurt caused by others is a sure way to get stuck in the past. Don't worry if the hurt is so great that you wonder where to get the strength to forgive. Where do you begin to forgive someone who took your mother's life right in front of you; or someone who raped you and infected you with an incurable disease; or that bully in grade 6 that wounded your self-esteem so badly that even at 54 you can't hold your head up high? This is where faith in God comes in. Believe that the Lord will provide the strength you need to let go of the extra weight that is unforgiveness.

The way I was able to forgive was, I embraced God's forgiveness of me. I understood that I had not been perfect. I had done wrong by not living my life for Christ. But God loved me anyway, so much that he gave his only son for me. He did it so that I would have an opportunity to live forever. I am only here by the grace of God, not by any great thing I have done. When you realize that, it humbles you.

I do understand that forgiveness is a process. The way we process it is to do it by Faith and not by feeling. We ask God for help daily. The more we work it out, the easier it becomes.

Step 4—Consider Counseling

A problem shared is half solved. Talking is so helpful that they made it into a profession. People spend years learning how to listen to people and extend help to them. These days, we have options in our spiritual leaders, clinical counseling with psychologists, marriage counseling, and so on. Seek God for direction and schedule an appointment with your primary care doctor.

If you are experiencing depression or anxiety or even PTSD there are many options for treatment and counseling available. They can evaluate you and recommend several options for care. At the end of the book, I'll add a list of resources that can help. Get the help you need to be free and fruitful to continue to work out your God-given purpose on the earth.

We must also resist the urge to always be in control. I had decided at a young age that in order for me to protect myself and be safe, I needed to be in complete control of my life. The problem with that was I had no idea who I was, whose I was, and what plan God had for me. So I made it up along the way. We all know how that turned out. Letting God in is resting in the Lord.

> Then Jesus said, "Come to me, all of you who are weary and carry heavy burdens, and I will give you rest. Take my yoke upon you. Let me teach you, because I am humble and gentle at heart, and you will find rest for your souls. For my yoke is easy to bear, and the burden I give you is light." (Matthew 11:28)

When we have acknowledged that we need help and now we desire to let God in, we must come to him. We must submit to him and learn from him. Going for counseling is a good way to hear from God through the people we talk to. If we were doing a good job of hearing from God, we wouldn't be in a fix in the first place, so we have to submit to his voice be it through our spiritual leaders or therapists. When we do it his way, we get to rest in Him. He wants to show us how to work out our purpose. This is an important step on your road to recovery.

When we are open to counseling, God is able to work through the counsellor or therapist to help you deal with those things that have been hidden. The things that have caused us to feel stuck. The key is making sure the counselor you choose is someone that gives you wise counsel, but since there is no sure way of doing that, this is where complete trust in God for direction comes in.

Step 5—Make It Count

They say experience is the best teacher. It is true, but not everyone should have to learn by experience. If we have had the opportunity to learn something, we must be willing to use what we have endured to help someone else.

> And they overcame him by the blood of
> the Lamb, and by the word of their testimony.
> (Revelation 12:11)

Our testimony, the story of how we overcame our struggles and got to a higher place, is not just for us alone. You do not keep the lessons learned bottled up inside you—you share it. My spiritual father always tells us, "We are salt, we are light we are agents of change." Everything we have experienced can be used. God doesn't waste anything. He may not have caused it but he can use it for His Glory. The shame, guilt, and disappointment are not a life sentence.

When I was in the abusive marriage, I truly thought it was for life. I felt it was all my fault. If it had not been for the grace of God, I would not have had the strength to leave. We can't allow embarrassment to stop us from being open and transparent about what we have been through so that others can learn from it. The Holy Spirit will lead and direct you when and where to share your testimony. The enemy would tell you to not let anyone know your business. He would tell you that they will judge you. The fact is, there is a strong possibility that they want to know the God that helped you make it through. We are all dealing with something. We live on three planes: we are spirits that live in bodies and we have souls. We function in five areas: spirit, soul, body, social, and financial. There are always areas with opportunity for improvement. There are also people who seem as though they have it all together, but you don't know their story. You always have to remember that.

God uses us to shine his light on the earth. We bring light into the darkness.

> Ye are the salt of the earth: but if the salt
> have lost his savour, wherewith shall it be salted?
> It is thenceforth good for nothing, but to be cast
> out, and to be trodden under foot of men. Ye are

the light of the world. A city that is set on an hill cannot be hid. Neither do men light a candle, and put it under a bushel, but on a candlestick; and it giveth light unto all that are in the house. Let your light so shine before men, that they may see your good works, and glorify your Father which is in heaven. (Matthew 5:13–16)

When we let our light shine, it attracts those that are in darkness. It draws attention not just to us, but the God in us. Making it count is using what was meant to destroy you to save someone else. This does not mean that we alone can save others, but we can point them to the one who can. We can save them from feeling alone, stuck, and left in their pain.

Find a way to give back. Volunteer to help those that have been hurt and victimized. You can make a difference. God doesn't cause the bad that happens to you, but he deserves the glory that comes out of it. When you overcome by faith and stand up against fear, shame, and abuse, you will touch and change lives with your story.

Change the Narrative

In closing, the steps above are how we change our story.

In the end, we are no longer the victim; we are victorious through Christ Jesus. We didn't just go through the trauma, we grew through the trauma. The things we experienced caused us to stretch and grow. We grew closer to the Lord. We grew by his love and his mercy that kept us.

Only by the grace of God will we stop replaying the incidents in our minds and feeling defeated. In the end, we can give God a shout of praise that we made it through. We now are ready for now what? We are ready to embrace the new things God has in store for us, moving ahead with the Lord.

These things that happened to me grew me so God could flow through me. And, in actuality, although it happened to me, I will not make it about me. Therefore, my testimony won't end with me—this is me making it our testimony. For every victim of rape, domestic abuse, and prostitution out there, this is our story of triumph.

I wasn't the first and unfortunately, I won't be the last. But I will be an example of how we overcome by the Blood of the lamb and the power of our testimony.

CHAPTER 7

Get Your Power Back

No matter what has happened in your past, it's time to get your power back.

One of the biggest things that stops us from moving forward is fear. You may have heard the acronym of fear being said to be False Evidence Appearing Real. It's true. How fear works is, it amplifies our doubts and magnifies the things we dread the most. It makes those things look so big that, even though they are only a figment of our imagination, they begin to seem real. Allowing fear to have a breeding ground in our hearts is an error we need to stop making.

The word of God says, "God gave us a spirit not of fear but of power and love and self-control." Fear does not come from God. The enemy uses fear to paralyze us and stop us from moving into our destiny in the Lord. The fear I am speaking of is the hesitation to move forward because you may doubt yourself; or not feel you desire greatness. All those lies come from the father of lies and his name is satan. He plays on our emotions to keep us in bondage—lost in the memories of all our mistakes, and errors. But from this day forth, we are taking back our power.

You have to realize, there is power in your assignment—your destiny...your calling—because it comes from God. We were created in the image and the likeness of God. He lives on the inside of us and it is from him that we draw strength. As a result, we cannot afford to be unplugged from our power source. Just like your phone needs to be plugged into a power source to charge so it could reach its full

IT HAPPENED NOW WHAT?

potential, so must we be plugged in and synced with the Lord. The goal is to achieve His will and His way.

Philippians 4:13 tells us that we can do all things through Christ who strengthens us. Therefore, we can dream again, live again, and love again no matter what the past looks like. There are no limits when we do it God's way. That's why we need to truly forget our past and look forward to the future God promises. We must forget the old to have space for the new.

> Forget what happened in the past, and do
> not dwell on events from long ago. I am going to
> do something new. It is already happening. Don't
> you recognize it? I will clear a way in the desert.
> I will make rivers on dry land. (Isaiah 43:18–19)

God is doing a new thing! He has cleared a way in the desert. In the dry places of our lives; in the embarrassing, shameful places of our memory, a change is coming. He wants to water those areas with rivers, hydrate those dry desolate areas, and spring forth a beautiful garden where once stood a wilderness. We must allow Him to do it. When we let Him in, we make way for his power to fill us and have control.

Getting our power back doesn't mean we are perfect and we won't endure more challenges. It means that we are in the process of perfection. We are moving on to now what? Now, what do you have for us, Lord? Now, who is it that needs to hear our stories? Now, who needs to know that they are not alone, that they don't have to stay in their current condition?

We are as the Apostle Paul declared in Philippians 3:13–14:

> I'm not saying that I have this all together,
> that I have it made. But I am well on my way,
> reaching out for Christ, who has so wondrously
> reached out for me. Friends, don't get me wrong:
> By no means do I count myself an expert in all of
> this, but I've got my eye on the goal, where God

is beckoning us onward—to Jesus. I'm off and running, and I'm not turning back.

We are promised in Romans 8:28:

> We know that all things work together for the good of those who love God—those whom he has called according to his plan.

Let us trust His plan and allow his power to work in and through us.

Resources

Victims of rape:
National Sexual Assault hotline—800-656-4673

Human trafficking:
Erase Child Trafficking hotline—800-819-3727

Domestic violence:
National Domestic Violence hotline—1-800-799-7233

Counseling:

- Faithful Counseling (www.faithfulcounseling.com)
- Regain Counseling (www.regain.us)
- Better Help Counseling (www.betterhelp.com)

SUBSTANCE USE

Substance Abuse and Mental Health Services Administration (SAMHSA)

- https://www.samhsa.gov

Alcoholics Anonymous

- https://aa.org

Narcotics Anonymous

- https://www.narcotics.com

ANXIETY DISORDERS

National Center for PTSD

- https://www.ptsd.va.gov

International OCD Foundation

- https://iocdf.org

Anxiety Disorders Association of America

- https://adaa.org

The Child Anxiety Network

- www.childanxiety.net

ATTENTION-DEFICIT HYPERACTIVITY DISORDER

ADDA – Attention Deficit Disorder Association

- https://add.org

NIMH, Attention-Deficit Hyperactivity Disorder

- https://www.nimh.nih.gov/health/topics/attention-deficit-hyperactivity-disorder-adhd/index.shtml

CHILD ABUSE AND DOMESTIC VIOLENCE

Georgia Coalition Against Domestic Violence

- https://gcadv.org

SAMSHA's Children and Families

- https://www.samhsa.gov/families

The National Domestic Violence Hotline • (800) 799-7233 (SAFE) • (800) 787-3224 (TTY)

- https://ncadv.org/get-help

CRISIS

- Georgia Crisis and Access Line (GCAL) • BHL (800) 715-4225 • Open 24/7
- Tennessee Statewide Crisis Line (855) 274-7471 • Open 24/7
- United Way Worldwide • dial 211 or visit https://www.unitedway.org
- Veterans Crisis Line (800) 273-8255 • Veterans Text 838255 • TTY (800) 799-4889

DEPRESSION DISORDERS

Depression-National Institute of Mental Health Information Line

- https://www.nimh.nih.gov/health/topics/depression

Depression and Bipolar Support Alliance

- https://www.dbsalliance.org

EATING DISORDERS

National Association of Anorexia Nervosa and associated disorders

- https://anad.org

National Eating Disorders Association

- https://www.nationaleatingdisorders.org

GRIEF AND LOSS

GriefShare

- https://www.griefshare.org

TRAUMA AND VIOLENCE

SAMSHA's Trauma and Violence

- https://www.samhsa.gov/trauma-violence

SUICIDE AWARENESS AND HOTLINES

SAMHSA's Suicide Prevention

- https://www.samhsa.gov/find-help/suicide-prevention

National Suicide Prevention Lifeline

- https://suicidepreventionlifeline.org

American Association of Suicidality

- https://suicidology.org

PSYCHOTHERAPY SERVICES

For Individual, Groups and Family Therapy Services, please contact your insurance company for a list of In Network Providers [INN]; If an INN provider is not available, please discuss the option of receiving services from an Out of Network [OON] provider paid at the INN rate.

Disclaimer: Kimcherian Johnson is not responsible for the content on the above listed sites.

SCRIPTURES FOR REFLECTION
AND APPLICATION

1 Peter 5:7 TPT

Pour out all your worries and stress upon him and leave them there, for he always tenderly cares for you.

Hebrews 10:23 TPT

So now we must cling tightly to the hope that lives within us, knowing that God always keeps his promises!

1 Corinthians 4:13 KJV

I can do all things through Christ which strengtheneth me.

Proverbs 3:5–6 TPT

Trust in the Lord completely, and do not rely on your own opinions. With all your heart rely on him to guide you, and he will lead you in every decision you make. Become intimate with him in whatever you do, and he will lead you wherever you go.

Psalm 3:3 KJV

But thou, O LORD, art a shield for me; my glory, and the lifter up of mine head.

1 Corinthians 15:57 NIV

But thanks be to God! He gives us the victory through our Lord Jesus Christ.

About the Author

Kimcherian Johnson is a minister, author, life coach, and global encourager. She uses her previous experiences, trauma, abuse, and disappointments as the fundament to inspire others to move beyond their pain and take back their power.

She is the founder of Empowered by HIM Book Connection and the co-founder of a global, Christian-based, life connection group entitled PURE Partners.

She also serves professionally as the Co-founder of PURE Coaching and development where she is a life coach and mentor alongside her husband, Elder Maurice Johnson I.

Kimcherian has been married to the love of her life for over twenty-two years and is blessed with five adult children and five grandchildren and one godson. She serves alongside her husband, Elder Maurice Johnson, under the leadership of Apostle Harold K. and Prophetess Gwen Browning of Faith Mission Ministries Inc. They are also a part of the Global Network of Christian Churches (GNCC).

Kim's ultimate goal is to provide encouragement, direction, and support in the lives of those who may have lost their power and passion. Her leadership and direction bring comfort and clarity to realign others with the plan of God for their lives.

CPSIA information can be obtained
at www.ICGtesting.com
Printed in the USA
BVHW072005130721
611841BV00002B/369